Margaret Atwood is the author of more than forty works, including fiction, poetry and critical essays, and her books have been published in over thirty-five countries. Of her novels, *The Blind Assassin* won the 2000 Booker Prize and *Alias Grace* won the Giller Prize in Canada and the Premio Mondello in Italy. Margaret Atwood's most recent novel is *MaddAddam* (2013). In 2005 she was the recipient of the Edinburgh Book Festival Enlightenment Award, for a distinguished contribution to world literature and thought. In 2008, Margaret Atwood was awarded the Prince of Asturias Prize for Literature in Spain. She lives in Toronto.

For more information, visit www.margaretatwood.ca

ALSO BY MARGARET ATWOOD

MARGARET ATWOOD

MURDER IN THE DARK

virago

VIRAGO

Published by Virago 1994
First published in Great Britain by Jonathan Cape Ltd 1984
This edition published by Virago Press in 2010

9 10 8

A CIP catalogue record for this book
is available from the British Library.

ISBN 978-1-84408-695-5

Typeset in Bembo by M Rules
Printed and bound in Great Britain by
Clays Ltd, St Ives plc

Papers used by Virago are from well-managed forests
and other responsible sources.

MIX
Paper from
responsible sources
FSC
www.fsc.org   FSC® C104740

Virago
An imprint of
Little, Brown Book Group
Carmelite House
50 Victoria Embankment
London EC4Y 0DZ

An Hachette UK Company
www.hachette.co.uk

www.virago.co.uk

CONTENTS

MURDER IN THE DARK

I

Autobiography

The first thing I can remember is a blue line. This was on the left, where the lake disappeared into the sky. At that point there was a white sand cliff, although you couldn't see it from where I was standing.

On the right the lake narrowed to a river and there was a dam and a covered bridge, some houses and a white church. In front there was a small rock island with a few trees on it. Along the shore there were large boulders and the sawed-off trunks of huge trees coming up through the water.

Behind is a house, a path running back into the forest, the entrance to another path which cannot be seen from where I was standing but was there anyway. At one spot this path was wider; oats fallen from the nosebags of loggers' horses during some distant winter had sprouted and grown. Hawks nested there.

Once, on the rock island, there was the half-eaten carcass of a deer, which smelled like iron, like rust rubbed into your hands so that it mixes with sweat. This smell is the point at which the landscape dissolves, ceases to be a landscape and becomes something else.

Making Poison

When I was five my brother and I made poison. We were living in a city then, but we probably would have made the poison anyway. We kept it in a paint can under somebody else's house and we put all the poisonous things into it that we could think of: toadstools, dead mice, mountain ash berries which may not have been poisonous but looked it, piss which we saved up in order to add it to the paint can. By the time the can was full everything in it was very poisonous.

The problem was that once having made the poison we couldn't just leave it there. We had to do something with it. We didn't want to put it into anyone's food, but we wanted an object, a completion. There was no one we hated enough, that was the difficulty.

I can't remember what we did with the poison in the end. Did we leave it under the corner of the house, which was made of wood and brownish yellow? Did we throw it at someone, some innocuous child? We wouldn't have dared an adult. Is this a true image I have, a small face streaming with tears and red berries, the sudden knowledge that the poison was really poisonous after all? Or did we throw it out, do I remember those red berries floating down a gutter, into a culvert, am I innocent?

Why did we make the poison in the first place? I can remember the glee with which we stirred and added, the sense of magic and accomplishment. Making poison is as much fun as making a cake. People like to make poison. If you don't understand this you will never understand anything.

The Boys' Own Annual, 1911

was in my grandfather's attic, along with a pump organ
that contained bats, rafter-high piles of Western paper-
backs, and a dress form, my grandmother's body frozen
in wire when it still had a waist. The attic smelled of dry
rot and smoked eels but it had a window, where the sunlight was yellower than anywhere else, because of the
dust maybe. This buttery sunlight framed the echoing
African caves where the underground streams ran, light-
less, haunted by crocodiles, white and eyeless, guarding
the entrance to the tunnel carved with Egyptian hiero-
glyphs and armed with deadly snakes and spiky
ambushes planted two thousand years ago to protect the

chamber of the sacred pearl, which for some reason, in stories like this, was always black. And when the hero snatched it out of the stone forehead looming bulbous and idolatrous there in the darkness, *filthy* was a word they liked, for other religions, the goddess was mad as blazes. Sinister priests with scimitars abounded, they could sniff you out like bloodhounds, their bare feet making no sound, until suddenly there was a set piece and down the hill went everyone, bounding along, loving it, yelling like crazy, bullets thudding into bodies into the scrub, into the surf, onto the waiting ship where Britain stood firm for plunder.

The issue with the last instalment had never come; it wasn't in the attic. So there I was, suspended in mid-story, in 1951, and there I remain, sometime, waiting for the end, or finishing it off myself, in a booklined London study over a stiff brandy, a yarn spun to a few choice gentlemen under the stuffed water buffalo head, a cheer-ful fire in the grate, or somewhere on the veldt, a bullet in the heart, who can tell where such greedy impulses will lead? Such lust for blind white crocodiles. In those times there were still chiefs in ostrich feathers and ene-mies worth killing, and loyalty, or so the story said.

Through the attic window and its golden dust and fly-husks I could see the barn, unpainted, hay coming out like stuffing from the loft doorway, and around the corner of it my grandmother's cow. She'd hook you if she could, if you didn't have a pitchfork. She was sneaking up on someone invisible; possibly my half uncle, gassed in the first war and never right since. The books had been his once.

Before the War

In the old days, before the war, things were different. You could walk out to the end of the dock any day around five and cast a couple of times and there would be your walleye, for supper or breakfast, hang it all night from a tree branch so the bears wouldn't get it, there were more bears then, they'd hang around the logging camps, you could go to the garbage dumps in the evenings and shoot them, I knew a man used a bow and arrow, not so good if you missed, more like real hunting though, he'd follow the trail of blood into the woods. They don't have logging camps now, not the way they used to, in winter, with horses to drag the trees to the ice, then in spring they'd tow them, in a boom, shoot them down river to the sawmill . It was swede saws and a double bitted axe, you can't get a good one any more, once they forget how to make them it'd take you years to teach anyone and there isn't the demand. They use trucks and bulldozers now, go in and level the place, hell of a mess, stumps and dead branches everywhere and no fish left to speak of; they fly in anyway now, in planes, something's happened to the Indians too, they never used to drink in the bush, it was always whites drank in the bush and the Indians drank in town, the bush was too important for them to take the risk of getting drunk in it, too drunk and you set a fire. In those days every man turned out to fight a fire, if there was one you turned out. In a wind it would jump the crowns, cross islands even. You'd work, you'd sweat for days without sleep to stop that fire.

Now they set them on purpose to get the work. Nobody cares, it's just a place to chew up the water with your speed-boat on the weekends. It was wooden boats they made themselves and a five horsepower motor, in the old days before the war.

The sun goes down, in the west as always, peach-coloured clouds, there's a shiver. It feels like waiting, but it isn't. Not a sound but the wind, the soft trickle of the small waves under the dock. There's no one here. One step off the path and there's never been anyone here, you think perhaps wrongly that it could all still be saved, even now. This is the old days. This is before the war.

Horror Comics

When I was twelve my friend C. and I used to pinch horror comics from the racks in drugstores. They were only ten cents then. We would read them on the way home from school, dramatizing the different parts, in radio voices with sound effects, to show we were above it. The blood was too copious and lurid, the faces were green and purple, the screams overdone. We leaned against the low stone wall outside the funeral home, laughing so much that C., whose mother said she should never use the school toilets for fear of catching some unspecified disease, had to cross her legs and beg me to stop.

'I'm really a vampire, you know,' I'd say in a conversational tone as we walked along, licking our lime popsicles. Those we paid for.

'No you aren't,' C. said, her voice uncertain.

'You know I am,' I said quietly. 'You don't have to be afraid of me though. You're my friend.' I dropped my voice an octave. 'I'm really dead, you know.'

'Stop it,' said C.

'Stop what?' I said innocently. 'I'm only telling you the truth.'

This occupied the four blocks between the funeral parlour and the gas station. After that we would switch to boys.

In winter, when it was dark after school, we threw snowballs at grownups, from behind, being careful to miss, doubling up with laughter because they didn't even know they were being aimed at. Once we even hit someone, a middle-aged woman in a muskrat coat. She turned around and looked at us, white-faced and glaring. We ran away, shrieking with guilty laughter, and threw ourselves backwards into a snowbank around the corner, holding our stomachs.

'The look on her face!' we screamed.

But we were terrified. It was the look on her face, pure hatred, real after all. The undead walked among us.

Boyfriends

Once I made my own clothes. What drove me to it, those seams endlessly sewn and ripped out and sewn again, the index finger needlepointed, thread all over the floor? I was fifteen. It was the princess line then, poured against the mid-riff, down into a gored skirt, the breasts fluffed out above.

The dress I remember is pink. I'm walking in it across a field, shopping centre to the right, hill to the left with its hard line of square brick houses. I'm carrying books, and a notebook, *binders* they were called. Between my left arm and the houses walks another person, a boy-friend, not touching me. I can't remember his name or what he looked like. It's the dress I remember, and the fact that when it was too old or too small for me I cut off the gold button from the front and kept it, and threw the dress away. The boyfriend exists too, but as an area of darkness. Not in the sense of sinister, a shadow merely, under a tree, a smell you can't identify, leather and banana peels or the vestibules of old movie houses, a whiff of the future. All I can see is the feet in their white and blue sneakers.

Another boyfriend, one I'm dancing with. It's later because the dress is red, I can see that all right, the skirt flaring out on either side of his legs: I'm looking down. The boyfriend himself is a blur, because I've taken off my glasses, as I always did to go out. I never did know what he really looked like, and he never knew what I really looked like, during the day, when I could see. In those days I groped my way through the world of evening men by touch and smell alone, purblind with vanity. At arms' length the boyfriends were shapes, solid at the core, misty around the edges and shining in the light from the streetlamps falling through the windows of the parked car. It was spring, everything was dense even after sunset with the smell of warm mud and the full moon, saturated with aftershave and breathing. The boyfriends were always slightly damp.

Up close they dissolved into texture, two square inches of skin, a fly's view, every hair distinct, both clearer and more obscure. At those times it was their aureoles I missed, reaching my hand into that dim fuzzy egg of light and encountering only stuffed cloth, grey at that. What was I looking at? Like Mars from a landed rocket, they no longer shone.

The Victory Burlesk

I went to the Victory Burlesk twice, or maybe it was only once and one of my friends went the other time and told me about it. I enjoyed it both times. It was considered quite daring for young women to go to such a place, and we thought it was funny; it was almost as funny as church.

You got a stand-up comic, a movie and a man who sang or juggled plates, as well as the strip-tease act. They used a lot of coloured lighting, red and blue and purple. Each girl had a fake name: Miss Take, Miss Behave, Flame LeRew. I liked the names and the costumes, for their ingenuity, and I liked the more skillful girls, the ones who could twirl tassles or make their bellies or buttocks rotate in a circle. That was before they had to take it all off, there was an art to it, it was almost like the plate juggling. I liked the way they floated in the pools of coloured light, moving as if they were swimming, mermaids behind glass.

One woman began with her back to the audience, the spotlight on her. She was wearing long white gloves and a black evening gown with gauzy black sleeves that looked like membranous wings as she stretched out her arms. She did a lot with her arms and back; but when she finally turned around, she was old. Her face was powdered dead white, her mouth was a bright reddish purple, but she was old. I could feel shame washing through me, it was no longer funny, I didn't want this woman to take off her clothes, I didn't want to look. I felt that I, not the woman on the stage, was being exposed and humiliated. Surely they would jeer and yell things at her, surely they would feel they had been tricked.

The woman unzipped her black evening gown, slipping it down, and began to move her hips. She smiled with her white mask of a face and her purple mouth, inside her lips her teeth glinted, dull white pebbles, it was a mockery, she didn't intend it, she knew it, it was a trick of another kind but we didn't know who was playing it. The trick was that suddenly there was no trick: the body up there was actual, it was aging, it was not floating in the spotlight somewhere apart from us, like us it was caught in time.

The Victory Burlesk went dead. Nobody made a sound.

Fainting

You're upright, standing on two feet in the usual way, and then suddenly you have a different point of view, the roots of the trees instead of the leafy tops, closeup of the floorboards, with nothing in between but a narrowing down and a rushing sound which is like wings but not the wings of angels.

The first time I was nine, in a crowd of winter coats in a Victorian building, steam-heated, looking at a display of chicken embryos, one day, five days, each one stopped short and bottled. There were twins too, human ones, identical and fraternal, their arteries and veins injected with coloured rubber, the purple sea-fan placenta, greyish now, in with them. After that I was looking up at a forest of canvas overshoes and legs. I could not remember folding or the moment when my head hit the wooden floor.

The other time I was carrying a basket of broken glass along a dock and I tripped and fell and cut my finger to the bone. I sat up and looked in, to my own body; there was no blood for a moment and I could see, it really was to the bone because there was the bone, not far down at all, shining up at me, white as an eyeball. I was older then so I put the basket down as soon as I heard those wings. The cut was right where the finger bends so there was no scar later, which I missed. You want to have something to show for it.

Worse things have happened since but the dark bird stays away. You faint when there's something you don't want to see, you can't bear to see. Someday, the bird calls from its leafless tree very far away, in the land where there is no sun and no moon, I will be back, and by then you will find me merciful.

Raw Materials

MUSIC Why do we travel? In other words, what are we doing here? Not much chance of a tan, it's foggy, it's the offseason. Those who want romance are over by the bar, being serenaded by three men with very loud voices and musical instruments made of wood. Those of us who want instead the real experience, whatever it may turn out to be, are out here, sitting at little tables and doggedly eating shrimp from newspaper packets, squeezing lime on them and dipping them in salt, almost like experts, natives, while the grey sea sweats in the background. The real experience, that's what we want, which means mescal with an authentic worm in the bottle. Still, you never know who you can trust. The worm could be faked.

This man doesn't want romance or the real experience either. He's here on business, he just wants someone to talk to. English, as he puts it. That's me all right, though he doesn't even like the shrimp. He's young, thirty, I asked, with beautiful teeth and a blond moustache and a chin that doesn't quite live up to the teeth. He smiles most of the time and has eyes that the naive might think of as candid. The accent suggests hound dogs and bourbon but he keeps it under control. He keeps everything well under control. He's gone through one wife already, he tells me, he was away too much. There's a lot of pressure.

This is his day off. Tomorrow he has to go elsewhere, to a nearby town. A ship's master has disappeared. He was seen entering a whorehouse but he was not seen coming out. This man has to check out all the whorehouses in town, to find the right one. If the ship's master can't be located, dead or alive, the widow gets a million dollars, which naturally the ship-owners would rather not pay unless they have to.

Isn't it dangerous? I say.

A whorehouse is the safest place around, he says. They have a reputation to keep up. I always get a policeman to go with me.

Then what? I say.

Mostly you just keep going till you dig up someone who knows the story, he says. Then you find out how much they want for it.

You mean bribery? I say, being from further north.

That's how it works, he says. That's how everything works. I like the Arabs, they're right out on the table. They even write it down for you: how much they want and for what. You don't have to pussyfoot around. Down here they make you guess, and if you guess wrong one way or the other they're insulted. Either that or they think you're a fool.

Aren't you ever afraid? I say. Do you carry a gun?

If I get scared I get out, he says. I get scared a lot and I get out a lot. Nothing's worth your life. He's not saying this to be impressive, it's merely what he thinks.

But you must like the travel, I say, hoping to redeem something for him.

He smiles a little, there isn't much he likes. It's work, he says.

I eat another shrimp, peeling it tail-first, wondering if this conversation counts as a real experience. There's a musician coming towards us, he thinks we're lovers, very soon we will be inundated by expensive sound.

A BEGGAR How was the food? they'll say when you get back. Indescribable, you'll say, and then you'll proceed to describe it, which will amuse everyone. There is food, of course, though not always what's expected. Try, for instance, to buy a pineapple.

We're sitting around a tin table in the heat, drinking local beer and eating a mutation, a kind of raisin bun. Hanging on the wall behind us is a display demonstrating different kinds of knots. An old brown man comes in, shuffling in a way we find theatrical. He has only two teeth left and he needs a shave.

He smiles and wants to shake hands with everyone. We shake hands with him, all three of us, and smile. Possibly he can't talk, or possibly he's pretending he can't. In any case, he makes a fist, to indicate (I think) marriage or sexual union, and points to my friend, then to the man I'm with. He's got it wrong and we correct him, smiling all the time. He nods and does it all over again and everyone smiles furiously. We've always gone for the real experience but there's something to be said for package tours.

He touches my shoulder and rubs the fingers of his right hand together. We aren't sure what this means; we discuss it. He turns away impatiently and goes to the doorway, where he stands with his back to us.

I think he wants money, I say. Isn't it bad luck not to give money to beggars?

His bent back is suddenly ominous. Who can tell what he's thinking, what ill wishes he's sending our way? We rummage for coins and find some, holding them in our hands just in case, and when he drifts our way – now he's making the rounds – we give them to him before he even asks. We're safe again.

But when our man, our protection, has left the table to pay the bill, the beggar comes back. He wants the remains of one of the awful buns, which lies on the plate chewed and soggy like something at a rained-out picnic. He points to the bun, then to himself. I give the bun to him and he takes it to the doorway to eat it.

Now we're gathering bags and cameras, scraping back our chairs. The beggar is here again, elbowing in amongst us, more urgent than before. He isn't smiling this time, he wants more and more. When will it stop? If we aren't careful he'll follow us to the hotel, climb walls, shove himself onto the plane with us, turn up some day on our front lawn. He's refusing to play beggar any more, he isn't letting us play tourists, embarrassed but benevolent, he's making us angry, this is too much.

Go away, we say. We make shooing motions with our hands, as if he's a bird. He smiles again, slipping back into his role, his costume, his wide grin of an idiot saint, two teeth, a mouthful of innocence and cunning. He's almost relieved. He's gone.

How was the food? they'll say. Monotonous, you'll say. There was a lot of chicken. Don't eat the salads, you'll get the glotch. Don't drink the water.

PALENQUE I am afraid of heights but not of small dark spaces. You are afraid of small dark spaces but not of heights. What better place for us to go?

Tonight it's chicken, *pollo*, the first word I learned, in chocolate sauce, and French fries, which like dandelions have infiltrated everywhere. We pay double what the man sitting next to us pays. He is not only local but the police chief, he keeps his revolver on while he eats. The chicken skidding about on my plate in brown mud is the same as all the other chickens we saw, through the train window, also skidding about in brown mud, chased by dogs which in turn were chased by little boys who in turn were chased by women in long white embroidered dresses I haven't yet learned to price at the market, under trees greener than green in the rain. Through the glass it looked idyllic.

In the morning we climb through steam rising everywhere from the plants, up the hill, scorning the tourist buses which pass us once in a while, not even full. Will it be worth it? we think. *Worth it* is what you get in relation to the discomfort you've invested. Whatever it is will have to make up for the bites, mosquito and flea, and the sawdust sandwiches on the train which everyone else knew better than to buy.

And here it is, one temple after another, miniature, perfect, almost alive still. But the steps are too steep, they were made so that you could never turn your back on the god, I can't climb them. It's not that I'm afraid of falling: heights go to my head, I start to believe I can really fly.

Just keep looking ahead, you say. Don't look behind you. You'll be all right.

But I don't believe it, I stay on the ground watching you go up and up, towards what? Something real. Envy impels me, I go around to the back, it's not so bad here, I scramble up a mudslide and make it to the top.

There's not much left up here but architecture and the minor messes of tourists. But now it's your turn: steps that go down, inside the pyramid, towards the deepest and most exciting tomb in the guidebook. It's dark and narrow and your knees start to give out. Holding hands, slipping on the wet stone, we descend.

This is where the slaves or wives were killed and left to guard the door, this was the door, blocked in; this is the final chamber. But they've taken everything out, the king, his extra golden face, the jade immortalizing him, it's all in a museum a thousand miles away. The tomb is empty, as they tend to be. That wasn't clear from the text.

What we remember is not the absent king but the fear.

THE JAGUAR THRONE We're standing in line to see the Jaguar Throne. It's almost Christmas now and everything is crowded, including the monasteries converted to ten-dollar-a-room hotels and the washrooms crammed with feet, in pastel sandals and the smell of orange peels and other things, and the crumbling hilltop temples with their inner walls luxuriant with graffiti, but this is the last chance we may ever have. Who knows when we'll be passing this way again?

The Jaguar Throne is embedded in a pyramid. First you go through a narrow tunnel entered at ground level, a tunnel so narrow your shoulders touch each side, the old stone unpleasantly damp, with a skin on it like the skin on a stagnant pond. There is only one passageway. Those who have already seen the Jaguar Throne push past us on the way back, squeezing us against the skin of the wall, in their hurry to reach the outside air again. Eagerly we scan their faces: was it worth it?

There are a few small lightbulbs strung along the ceiling, a wire festooned between them. The ceiling itself is getting lower. The air is moist and dead. The line inches forward. Ahead of us there are backs, the necks sunburned, the shirts and dresses ringed with sweat beneath the arms. Nobody says anything, though the heavy air seems full of whispers. Ahead of us, up some steps, around corners, unseen, the Jaguar Throne crouches in a square cubicle, its ruby eyes glowing, its teeth vivid, its meaning lost. Who used it last, what was it for, why was it kept here, out of sight in the darkness?

The line of people moves forward into the absence of light. There must have been processions once, flames carried, dimming in the lack of oxygen, men in masks, willing or not. The Jaguar Throne was not always a curiosity, something to see at Christmas. Once there were gods who needed propitiation. Once they played a game here, in an outside court, with stone rings set into the walls. If your team lost they cut off your head. That's what the carving is, the body of a man with a fountain in place of the head: the blessed loser, making it rain. Metaphor can be dangerous. Not everyone wants to see the Jaguar Throne but some see it anyway.

Ahead of us a woman screams. Panic runs through the line, you can feel it jumping from body to body, there's a surge backwards: in a minute we'll be stampeded, crushed. Then comes the rumour, the whisper: it was only a spider. We're caught anyway, the tunnel's jammed, we can't move, we stand in the dead air listening to our hearts, and now we know the answer: the Jaguar Throne is kept in here so it can't get out.

THE WATER GOD A long time ago this cave was sealed up. From the pictures they left you can deduce when: they were drawing creatures with six legs and metal heads, monsters, the monsters were swimming ashore from their huge white-winged boats, marked with evil and bad luck. They were burning the people and killing them with their sticks that licked out fire. This is what it looks like in the drawings. Now they were coming south.

The priests did not want the monsters to find the cave and use it for their own purposes. They broke the sac-rificial bowls and the images of the gods, releasing their spirits. They left their baked clay breastplates of office lying shattered in the large cavern, the one with the cen-tral pillar smudged with handprints the colour of dried blood. They backed out of the cave, building walls as they went: one wall of cut stone and a second wall against which they piled rubble, to make it look like an accident, some shrug of the earth. Devoid of their magic, the priests disappeared into the people, whom they could no longer protect, who could not protect them, and like them they were butchered or enslaved.

Now we retrace their steps. In point of fact I would rather have stayed on the patio, in the yellow sunlight, drinking *café con leche* and watching the toucans in their cages, but in this country you are drawn to dark places. Bowing our heads, we pass through the first low doorway. The ceiling is not far above us, the roots of trees grow down through it, holding it in place. At the second doorway we must crawl.

Here is the entrance to the central cave, in which you can still smell fear and the oily light of torches. There are bowls at the foot of the pillar, masks, a face within a face, holes punched in them, the spirit gone. Branching off to the left is a corridor with a line of tiny altars: on each is a plate, no bigger than a doll's dish, and on each plate is a single grain of dusty corn, placed carefully so the people would eat that year. Everything is still the way it was left.

At the end of the corridor there's an underground spring, a shallow lake, the water clear as tears, tinged with blue. Pale blunt fish swim in it, probably blind. Out in the centre is the water god, sad-faced, floating on stone and twinned in the blue pool. We can't tell whether or not he's been broken. Possibly they thought the water god could take care of himself.

We walk back down the corridor, touching nothing, knowing that we have intruded, blundered upon a child's serious and profoundly believed game, and we have spoiled everything.

Murder in the Dark

This is a game I've played only twice. The first time I was in Grade Five, I played it in a cellar, the cellar of a large house belonging to the parents of a girl called Louise. There was a pool table in the cellar but none of us knew anything about pool. There was also a player piano. After a while we got tired of running the punch-card rolls through the player piano and watching the keys go up and down by themselves, like something in a late movie just before you see the dead person. I was in love with a boy called Bill, who was in love with Louise. The other boy, whose name I can't remember, was in love with me. Nobody knew who Louise was in love with.

So we turned out the lights in the cellar and played *Murder in the Dark*, which gave the boys the pleasure of being able to put their hands around the girls' necks and gave the girls the pleasure of screaming. The excitement was almost more than we could bear, but luckily Louise's parents came home and asked us what we thought we were up to.

The second time I played it was with adults; it was not as much fun, though more intellectually complex.

I heard that this game was once played at a summer cottage by six normal people and a poet, and the poet really tried to kill someone. He was hindered only by the intervention of a dog, which could not tell fantasy from reality. The thing about this game is that you have to know when to stop.

Here is how you play:

You fold up some pieces of paper and put them into a hat, a bowl or the centre of the table. Everyone chooses a piece. The one who gets the x is the detective, the one who gets the black spot is the killer. The detective leaves the room, turning off the lights. Everyone gropes around in the dark until the murderer picks a victim. He can either whisper, 'You're dead,' or he can slip his hands

48

around a throat and give a playful but decisive squeeze. The victim screams and falls down. Everyone must now stop moving around except the murderer, who of course will not want to be found near the body. The detective counts to ten, turns on the lights and enters the room. He may now question anyone but the victim, who is not allowed to answer, being dead. Everyone but the murderer must tell the truth. The murderer must lie.

If you like, you can play games with this game. You can say: the murderer is the writer, the detective is the reader, the victim is the book. Or perhaps, the murderer is the writer, the detective is the critic and the victim is the reader. In that case the book would be the total *mise en scène*, including the lamp that was accidentally tipped over and broken. But really it's more fun just to play the game.

In any case, that's me in the dark. I have designs on you, I'm plotting my sinister crime, my hands are reaching for your neck or perhaps, by mistake, your thigh. You can hear my footsteps approaching, I wear boots and carry a knife, or maybe it's a pearl-handled revolver, in any case I wear boots with very soft soles, you can see the cinematic glow of my cigarette, waxing and waning in the fog of the room, the street, the room, even though I don't smoke. Just remember this, when the scream at last has ended and you've turned on the lights: by the rules of the game, I must always lie.

Now: do you believe me?

Simmering

It started in the backyards. At first the men concentrated on heat and smoke, and on dangerous thrusts with long forks. Their wives gave them aprons in railroad stripes, with slogans on the front – *Hot Stuff*, *The Boss* – to spur them on. Then it began to get all mixed up with who should do the dishes, and you can't fall back on paper plates forever, and around that time the wives got tired of making butterscotch brownies and jello salads with grated carrots and baby marshmallows in them and wanted to make money instead, and one thing led to another. The wives said that there were only twenty-four hours in a day; and the men, who in that century were still priding themselves on their rationality, had to agree that this was so.

For a while they worked it out that the men were in charge of the more masculine kinds of food: roasts, chops, steaks, dead chickens and ducks, gizzards, hearts, anything that had obviously been killed, that had visibly bled. The wives did the other things, the glazed parsnips and the prune whip, anything that flowered or fruited or was soft and gooey in the middle. That was all right for about a decade. Everyone praised the men to keep them going, and the wives, sneaking out of the houses in the mornings with their squeaky new briefcases, clutching their bus tickets because the men needed the station wagons to bring home the carcasses, felt they had got away with something.

But time is not static, and the men refused to stay put. They could not be kept isolated in their individual kitchens, kitchens into which the wives were allowed less and less frequently because, the men said, they did not sharpen the knives properly, if at all. The men began to acquire kitchen machines, which they would spend the weekends taking apart and oiling. There were a few accidents at first, a few lost fingers and ends of noses, but the men soon got the hang of it and branched out into other areas: automatic nutmeg graters, electric gadgets for taking the lids off jars. At cocktail parties they would gather in groups at one end of the room, exchanging private recipes and cooking yarns, tales of soufflés daringly saved at the last minute, pears flambées which had gone out of control and had to be fought to a standstill. Some of these stories had risqué phrases in them, such as *chicken breasts*. Indeed, sexual metaphor was changing: bowls and forks became prominent, and *eggbeater*, *pressure cooker* and *turkey baster* became words which only the most daring young women, the kind who thought it was a kick to butter their own toast, would venture to pronounce in mixed company. Men who could not cook very well hung about the edges of these groups, afraid to say much, admiring the older and more experienced ones, wishing they could be like them.

Soon after that, the men resigned from their jobs in large numbers so they could spend more time in the kitchen. The magazines said it was a modern trend. The wives were all driven off to work, whether they wanted to or not: someone had to make the money, and of course they did not want their husbands' masculinity to be threatened. A man's status in the community was now displayed by the length of his carving knives, by how many of them he had and how sharp he kept them, and by whether they were plain or ornamented with gold and precious jewels.

Exclusive clubs and secret societies sprang up. Men meeting for the first time would now exchange special handshakes – the Béchamel twist, the chocolate mousse double grip – to show that they had been initiated. It was pointed out to the women, who by this time did not go into the kitchens at all on pain of being thought unfeminine, that *chef* after all means *chief* and that Mixmasters were common but no one had ever heard of a Mixmistress. Psychological articles began to appear in the magazines on the origin of women's kitchen envy and how it could be cured. Amputation of the tip of the tongue was recommended, and, as you know, became a widespread practice in the more advanced nations. If Nature had meant women to cook, it was said, God would have made carving knives round and with holes in them.

This is history. But it is not a history familiar to many people. It exists only in the few archival collections that have not yet been destroyed, and in manuscripts like this one, passed from woman to woman, usually at night, copied out by hand or memorized. It is subversive of me even to write these words. I am doing so, at the risk of my own personal freedom, because now, after so many centuries of stagnation, there are signs that hope and therefore change have once more become possible.

The women in their pinstripe suits, exiled to the living rooms where they dutifully sip the glasses of port brought out to them by the men, used to sit uneasily, silently, listening to the loud bursts of male and somehow derisive laughter from behind the closed kitchen doors. But they have begun whispering to each other. When they are with those they trust, they tell of a time long ago, lost in the fogs of legend, hinted at in packets of letters found in attic trunks and in the cryptic frescoes on abandoned temple walls, when women too were allowed to participate in the ritual which now embodies the deepest religious convictions of our society: the transformation of the consecrated flour into the holy bread. At night they dream, long clandestine dreams, confused and obscured by shadows. They dream of plunging their hands into the earth, which is red as blood and soft, which is milky and warm. They dream that the earth gathers itself under their hands, swells, changes its form, flowers into a thousand shapes, for them too, for them once more. They dream of apples; they dream of the creation of the world; they dream of freedom.

Women's Novels

FOR LENORE

1. Men's novels are about men. Women's novels are about men too but from a different point of view. You can have a men's novel with no women in it except possibly the landlady or the horse, but you can't have a women's novel with no men in it. Sometimes men put women in men's novels but they leave out some of the parts: the heads, for instance, or the hands. Women's novels leave out parts of the men as well. Sometimes it's the stretch between the belly button and the knees, sometimes it's the sense

of humour. It's hard to have a sense of humour in a cloak, in a high wind, on a moor.

Women do not usually write novels of the type favoured by men but men are known to write novels of the type favoured by women. Some people find this odd.

2. I like to read novels in which the heroine has a costume rustling discreetly over her breasts, or discreet breasts rustling under her costume; in any case there must be a costume, some breasts, some rustling, and, over all, discretion. Discretion over all, like a fog, a miasma through which the outlines of things appear only vaguely. A glimpse of pink through the gloom, the sound of breathing, satin slithering to the floor, revealing what? Never mind, I say. Never never mind.

3. Men favour heroes who are tough and hard: tough with men, hard with women. Sometimes the hero goes soft on a woman but this is always a mistake. Women do not favour heroines who are tough and hard. Instead they have to be tough and soft. This

leads to linguistic difficulties. Last time we looked, monosyllables were male, still dominant but sinking fast, wrapped in the octopoid arms of labial polysyllables, whispering to them with arachnoid grace: *darling, darling*.

4. Men's novels are about how to get power. Killing and so on, or winning and so on. So are women's novels, though the method is different. In men's novels, getting the woman or women goes along with getting the power. It's a perk, not a means. In women's novels you get the power by getting the man. The man is the power. But sex won't do, he has to love you. What do you think all that kneeling's about, down among the crinolines, on the Persian carpet? Or at least say it. When all else is lacking, verbalization can be enough. *Love*. There, you can stand up now, it didn't kill you. Did it?

5. I no longer want to read about anything sad. Anything violent, anything disturbing, anything like that. No funerals at the end, though there can be some in the middle. If there must be deaths, let

there be resurrections, or at least a Heaven so we know where we are. Depression and squalor are for those under twenty-five, they can take it, they even like it, they still have enough time left. But real life is bad for you, hold it in your hand long enough and you'll get pimples and become feebleminded. You'll go blind.

I want happiness, guaranteed, joy all round, covers with nurses on them or brides, intelligent girls but not too intelligent, with regular teeth and pluck and both breasts the same size and no excess facial hair, someone you can depend on to know where the bandages are and to turn the hero, that potential rake and killer, into a well-groomed country gentleman with clean fingernails and the right vocabulary. *Always*, he has to say. *Forever*. I no longer want to read books that don't end with the word *forever*. I want to be stroked between the eyes, one way only.

6. Some people think a woman's novel is anything without politics in it. Some think it's anything about relationships. Some think it's anything with a lot of operations in it, medical ones I mean. Some think it's

anything that doesn't give you a broad panoramic view of our exciting times. Me, well, I just want something you can leave on the coffee table and not be too worried if the kids get into it. You think that's not a real consideration? You're wrong.

7. *She had the startled eyes of a wild bird.* This is the kind of sentence I go mad for. I would like to be able to write such sentences, without embarrassment. I would like to be able to read them without embarrassment. If I could only do these two simple things, I feel, I would be able to pass my allotted time on this earth like a pearl wrapped in velvet.

She had the startled eyes of a wild bird. Ah, but which one? A screech owl, perhaps, or a cuckoo? It does make a difference. We do not need more literalists of the imagination. They cannot read a body like a gazelle's without thinking of intestinal parasites, zoos and smells.

She had a feral gaze like that of an untamed animal, I read. Reluctantly I put down the book, thumb still inserted at the exciting moment. He's about to crush her in his arms, pressing his hot, devouring, hard, demanding mouth to hers as her breasts squish out the top of her dress, but I can't concentrate. Metaphor leads me by the nose, into the maze, and suddenly all Eden lies before me. Porcupines, weasels, warthogs and skunks, their feral gazes malicious or bland or stolid or piggy and sly. Agony, to see the romantic *frisson* quivering just out of reach, a dark-winged butterfly stuck to an over-ripe peach, and not to be able to swallow, or wallow. *Which one?* I murmur to the unresponding air. *Which one?*

Happy Endings

John and Mary meet.

What happens next?

If you want a happy ending, try A.

A. John and Mary fall in love and get married. They both have worthwhile and remunerative jobs which they find stimulating and challenging. They buy a charming house. Real estate values go up. Eventually, when they can afford live-in help, they have two children, to whom they are devoted. The children turn out well. John and Mary have a stimulating and challenging sex life and worthwhile friends.

They go on fun vacations together. They retire. They both have hobbies which they find stimulating and challenging. Eventually they die. This is the end of the story.

B. Mary falls in love with John but John doesn't fall in love with Mary. He merely uses her body for selfish pleasure and ego gratification of a tepid kind. He comes to her apartment twice a week and she cooks him dinner, you'll notice that he doesn't even consider her worth the price of a dinner out, and after he's eaten the dinner he fucks her and after that he falls asleep, while she does the dishes so he won't think she's untidy, having all those dirty dishes lying around, and puts on fresh lipstick so she'll look good when he wakes up, but when he wakes up he doesn't even notice, he puts on his socks and his shorts and his pants and his shirt and his tie and his shoes, the reverse order from the one in which he took them off. He doesn't take off Mary's clothes, she takes them off herself, she acts as if she's dying for it every time, not because she likes sex exactly, she doesn't, but she wants John to think she does because if they do it often enough surely he'll get used to her, he'll come to depend on her and they will get married, but John goes out the door with hardly so much as a goodnight and three days later he turns up at six o'clock and they do the whole thing over again.

Mary gets run down. Crying is bad for your face, everyone knows that and so does Mary but she can't stop. People at work notice. Her friends tell her John is a rat, a pig, a dog, he isn't good enough for her, but she can't believe it. Inside John, she thinks, is another John, who is much nicer. This other John will emerge like a butterfly from a cocoon, a Jack from a box, a pit from a prune, if the first John is only squeezed enough.

One evening John complains about the food. He has never complained about the food before. Mary is hurt.

Her friends tell her they've seen him in a restaurant with another woman, whose name is Madge. It's not even Madge that finally gets to Mary: it's the restaurant. John has never taken Mary to a restaurant. Mary collects all the sleeping pills and aspirins she can find, and takes them and half a bottle of sherry. You can see what kind of a woman she is by the fact that it's not even whiskey. She leaves a note for John. She hopes he'll discover her and get her to the hospital in time and repent and then they can get married, but this fails to happen and she dies.

John marries Madge and everything continues as in A.

C. John, who is an older man, falls in love with Mary, and Mary, who is only twenty-two, feels sorry for him because he's worried about his hair falling out. She sleeps with him even though she's not in love with him. She met him at work. She's in love with someone called James, who is twenty-two also and not yet ready to settle down.

John on the contrary settled down long ago: this is what is bothering him. John has a steady respectable job and is getting ahead in his field, but Mary isn't impressed by him, she's impressed by James, who has a motorcycle and a fabulous record collection. But James is often away on his motorcycle, being free. Freedom isn't the same for girls, so in the meantime Mary spends Thursday evenings with John. Thursdays are the only days John can get away.

John is married to a woman called Madge and they have two children, a charming house which they bought just before the real estate values went up, and hobbies which they find stimulating and challenging, when they have the time. John tells Mary how important she is to him, but of course he can't leave his wife because a commitment is a commitment. He goes on about this more than is necessary and Mary finds it boring, but older men can keep it up longer so on the whole she has a fairly good time.

One day James breezes in on his motorcycle with some top grade California hybrid and James and Mary get higher than you'd believe possible and they climb into bed. Everything becomes very underwater, but along comes John, who has a key to Mary's apartment. He finds them stoned and entwined. He's hardly in any position to be jealous, considering Madge, but nevertheless he's overcome with despair. Finally he's middle-aged, in two years he'll be bald as an egg and he can't stand it. He purchases a handgun, saying he needs it for target practice – this is the thin part of the plot, but it can be dealt with later – and shoots the two of them and himself.

Madge, after a suitable period of mourning, marries an understanding man called Fred and everything continues as in A, but under different names.

D. Fred and Madge have no problems. They get along exceptionally well and are good at working out any little difficulties that may arise. But their charming house is by the seashore and one day a giant tidal wave approaches. Real estate values go down. The rest of the story is about what caused the tidal wave and how they escape from it. They do, though thousands drown. Some of the story is about how the thousands drown, but Fred and Madge are virtuous and lucky. Finally on high ground they clasp each other, wet and dripping and grateful, and continue as in A.

E. Yes, but Fred has a bad heart. The rest of the story is about how kind and understanding they both are

until Fred dies. Then Madge devotes herself to char-
ity work until the end of A. If you like, it can be
'Madge,' 'cancer,' 'guilty and confused,' and 'bird
watching'.

F. If you think this is all too bourgeois, make John a rev-
olutionary and Mary a counterespionage agent and
see how far that gets you. Remember, this is Canada.
You'll still end up with A, though in between you
may get a lustful brawling saga of passionate involve-
ment, a chronicle of our times, sort of.

————

You'll have to face it, the endings are the same however you slice it. Don't be deluded by any other
endings, they're all fake, either deliberately fake, with
malicious intent to deceive, or just motivated by
excessive optimism if not by downright sentimen-
tality.

The only authentic ending is the one provided
here:

John and Mary die. John and Mary die. John and Mary die.

———

So much for endings. Beginnings are always more fun. True connoisseurs, however, are known to favour the stretch in between, since it's the hardest to do anything with.

That's about all that can be said for plots, which anyway are just one thing after another, a what and a what and a what.

Now try How and Why.

Bread

Imagine a piece of bread. You don't have to imagine it, it's right here in the kitchen, on the bread board, in its plastic bag lying beside the bread knife. The bread knife is an old one you picked up at an auction; it has the word BREAD carved into the wooden handle. You open the bag, pull back the wrapper, cut yourself a slice. You put butter on it, then peanut butter, then honey, and you fold it over. Some of the honey runs out onto your fingers and you lick it off. It takes you about a minute to eat the bread. This bread happens to be brown, but there is also white bread, in the refrigerator, and a heel of rye you got last week, round as a full stomach then, now going mouldy. Occasionally you make bread. You think of it as something relaxing to do with your hands.

———

Imagine a famine. Now imagine a piece of bread. Both of these things are real but you happen to be in the same room with only one of them. Put yourself into a different room, that's what the mind is for. You are now lying on a thin mattress in a hot room. The walls are made of dried earth and your sister, who is younger than you are, is in the room with you. She is starving, her belly is bloated, flies land on her eyes; you brush them off with your hand. You have a cloth too, filthy but damp, and you press it to her lips and forehead. The piece of bread is the bread you've been saving, for days it seems. You are as hungry as she is, but not yet as weak. How long does this take? When will someone come with more bread? You think of going out to see if you might find some- thing that could be eaten, but outside the streets are infested with scavengers and the stink of corpses is everywhere.

Should you share the bread or give the whole piece to your sister? Should you eat the piece of bread yourself? After all, you have a better chance of living, you're stronger. How long does it take to decide?

———

Imagine a prison. There is something you know that you have not yet told. Those in control of the prison know that you know. So do those not in control. If you tell, thirty or forty or a hundred of your friends, your comrades, will be caught and will die. If you refuse to tell, tonight will be like last night. They always choose the night. You don't think about the night however, but about the piece of bread they offered you. How long does it take? The piece of bread was brown and fresh and reminded you of sunlight falling across a wooden floor. It reminded you of a bowl, a yellow bowl that was once in your home. It held apples and pears; it stood on a table you can also remember. It's not the hunger or the pain that is killing you but the absence of the yellow bowl. If you could only hold the bowl in your hands, right here, you could withstand anything, you tell yourself. The bread they offered you is subversive, it's treacherous, it does not mean life.

———

There were once two sisters. One was rich and had no children, the other had five children and was a widow, so poor that she no longer had any food left. She went to her sister and asked her for a mouthful of bread. 'My children are dying,' she said. The rich sister said, 'I do not have enough for myself,' and drove her away from the door. Then the husband of the rich sister came home and wanted to cut himself a piece of bread; but when he made the first cut, out flowed red blood.

Everyone knew what that meant.

This is a traditional German fairy-tale.

———

The loaf of bread I have conjured for you floats about a foot above your kitchen table. The table is normal, there are no trap doors in it. A blue tea towel floats beneath the bread, and there are no strings attaching the cloth to the bread or the bread to the ceiling or the table to the cloth, you've proved it by passing your hand above and below. You didn't touch the bread though. What stopped you? You don't want to know whether the bread is real or whether it's just a hallucination I've somehow duped you into seeing. There's no doubt that you can see the bread, you can even smell it, it smells like yeast, and it looks solid enough, solid as your own arm. But can you trust it? Can you eat it? You don't want to know, imagine that.

The Page

1. The page waits, pretending to be blank. Is that its appeal, its blankness? What else is this smooth and white, this terrifyingly innocent? A snowfall, a glacier? It's a desert, totally arid, without life. But people venture into such places. Why? To see how much they can endure, how much dry light?

2. I've said the page is white, and it is: white as wedding dresses, rare whales, seagulls, angels, ice and death. Some say that like sunlight it contains all colours; others, that it's white because it's hot, it will burn out

your optic nerves; that those who stare at the page too long go blind.

3. The page itself has no dimensions and no directions. There's no up or down except what you yourself mark, there's no thickness and weight but those you put there, north and south do not exist unless you're certain of them. The page is without vistas and without sounds, without centres or edges. Because of this you can become lost in it forever. Have you never seen the look of gratitude, the look of joy, on the faces of those who have managed to return from the page? Despite their faintness, their loss of blood, they fall on their knees, they push their hands into the earth, they clasp the bodies of those they love, or, in a pinch, any bodies they can get, with an urgency unknown to those who have never experienced the full horror of a journey into the page.

4. If you decide to enter the page, take a knife and some matches, and something that will float. Take something you can hold onto, and a prism to split the light and a talisman that works, which should be

hung on a chain around your neck: that's for getting back. It doesn't matter what kind of shoes, but your hands should be bare. You should never go into the page with gloves on. Such decisions, needless to say, should not be made lightly.

There are those, of course, who enter the page without deciding, without meaning to. Some of these have charmed lives and no difficulty, but most never make it out at all. For them the page appears as a well, a lovely pool in which they catch sight of a face, their own but better. These unfortunates do not jump: rather they fall and the page closes over their heads without a sound, without a seam, and is immediately as whole and empty, as glassy, as enticing as before.

5. The question about the page is: what is beneath it? It seems to have only two dimensions, you can pick it up and turn it over and the back is the same as the front. Nothing, you say, disappointed.

But you were looking in the wrong place, you were looking *on the back* instead of *beneath*. *Beneath the page* is another story. Beneath the page is a story.

Beneath the page is everything that has ever happened, most of which you would rather not hear about.

The page is not a pool but a skin, a skin is there to hold in and it can feel you touching it. Did you really think it would just lie there and do nothing?

Touch the page at your peril: it is you who are blank and innocent, not the page. Nevertheless you want to know, nothing will stop you. You touch the page, it's as if you've drawn a knife across it, the page has been hurt now, a sinuous wound opens, a thin incision. Darkness wells through.

IV

VI

Mute

Whether to speak or not: the question that comes up again when you think you've said too much, again. Another clutch of nouns, a fistful: look how they pick them over, the shoppers for words, pinching here and there to see if they're bruised yet. Verbs are no better, they wind them up, let them go, scrabbling over the table, wind them up again too tight and the spring breaks. You can't take another poem of spring, not with the wound-up vowels, not with the bruised word green in it, not yours, not with ants crawling all over it, not this infestation. It's a market, flyspecked; how do you wash a language? There's the beginning of a bad smell, you can hear the growls, something's being eaten, once too often. Your mouth feels rotted.

Why involve yourself? You'd do better to sit off to the side, on the sidewalk under the awning, hands over your mouth, your ears, your eyes, with a cup in front of you into which people will or will not drop pennies. They think you can't talk, they're sorry for you, but. But you're waiting for the word, the one that will finally be right. A compound, the generation of life, mud and light.

She

knows exactly what she's doing. Well, why not? Along the street, around the corner, the piece of her that's just disappearing. If that's the way it works, that's what she'll do. Sometimes in shorts, with tanned thighs, or with sleeves like cabbages, or the whole body falling liquid from the shoulders: whatever's about to happen. Lace at the throat, the ankle, skimming the breasts, wherever they're putting it this year, and a laugh or not, at the pulsepoint. What will it get her? Something. You have to know when to run and where, how to close a door, gently. Just a little showing, something that looks like flesh, they follow, a few white stones dropped in the forest, under the trees, shining in the moonlight, clues, a trail. To get from one point to the next and then see another, and another beyond that. She deals in longing, the sickness of the heart, stuttering of the arteries, would you call it suffering, where does it lead? Deeper into the forest, deeper into the moonlight. They think they'll come out from among the trees and she will be there, finally waiting, for them, all cool white light.

Worship

You have these sores in your mouth that will not heal. It's from eating too much sugar, you tell yourself. To the gods men offer flowers and food, remember those chrysanthemums, those pumpkins, at the altar, even in that square brick church? The one that smelled like wet feet, wearing socks, for a long time. Thanksgiving. That's why he brings you roses, on occasion, and chocolates when he can't think of anything else. For the same reasons too: worship or ritual or sucking up. Prayer is wanting. Jesus, Jesus he says, but he's not praying to Jesus, he's praying to you, not to your body or your face but to that space you hold at the centre, which is the shape of the universe. Empty. He wants response, an answer from that dark sphere and its red stars, which he can touch but not see. How does it feel to be a god, for five minutes anyway? Now you know what they have to put up with. Those groans that sound so much like suffering and perhaps are, you can't tell by listening.

You aren't really a god but despite that you are silent. When you're being worshipped there isn't much to say. It's White Gift Sunday, tinned goods this time, in tissue paper, for the poor, and that's you up there, shining, burning, like a candle, like a chalice, burnished; with use and service. After you've been serviced, after you've been used, you'll be put away again until needed.

Iconography

He wants her arranged just so. He wants her, arranged. He arranges to want her.

This is the arrangement they have made. With strings attached, or ropes, stockings, leather straps. What else is arranged? Furniture, flowers. For contemplation and a graceful disposition of parts to compose a unified and aesthetic whole.

Once she wasn't supposed to like it. To have her in a position she didn't like, that was power. Even if she liked it she had to pretend she didn't. Then she was supposed to like it. To make her do something she didn't like and then make her like it, that was greater power. The greatest power of all is when she doesn't really like it but she's supposed to like it, so she has to pretend.

Whether he's making her like it or making her dislike it or making her pretend to like it is important but it's not the most important thing. The most important thing is making her. Over, from nothing, new. From scratch, the way he wants.

It can never be known whether she likes it or not. By this time she doesn't know herself. All you see is the skin, that smile of hers, flat but indelible, like a tattoo. Hard to tell, and she never will, she can't. They don't get into it unless they like it, he says. He has the last word. He has the word.

Watch yourself. That's what the mirrors are for, this story is a mirror story which rhymes with horror story, almost but not quite. We fall back into these rhythms as if into safe hands.

Liking Men

It's time to like men again. Where shall we begin?

I have a personal preference for the backs of necks, because of the word *nape*, so lightly furred; which is different from the word *scruff*. But for most of us, especially the beginners, it's best to start with the feet and work up. To begin with the head and all it contains would be too suddenly painful. Then there's the navel, birth dimple, where we fell from the stem, something we have in common; you could look at it and say, He also is mortal. But it may be too close for comfort to those belts and zippers which cause you such distress, and comfort is what you want. He's a carnivore, you're a vegetarian. That's what you have to get over.

The feet then. I give you the feet, pinkly toed and innocuous. Unfortunately you think of socks, lying on the floor, waiting to be picked up and washed. Quickly add shoes. Better? The socks are now contained, and presumably clean.

You contemplate the shoes, shined but not too much – you don't want this man to be either a messy slob or prissy – and you begin to relax. Shoes, kind and civilized, not black but a decent shade of brown. No raucous two-tones, no elevator heels. The shoes dance, with the feet in them, neatly, adroitly, you enjoy this, you think of Fred Astaire, you're beginning to like men. You think of kissing those feet, slowly, after a good scrubbing of course; the feet expand their toes, squirm with pleasure. You like to give pleasure. You run your tongue along the sole and the feet moan.

Cheered up, you start fooling around. *Footgear*, you think. Golf shoes, grassy and fatherly, white sneakers for playing tennis in, agile and sweet, quick as rabbits. Workboots, solid and trustworthy. A good man is hard to find but they do exist, you know it now. Someone who can run a chainsaw without cutting off his leg. What a relief. Checks and plaids, laconic, a little Scottish. Rubber boots, for wading out to the barn in the rain in order to save the baby calf. Power, quiet and sane. Knowing what to do, doing it well. Sexy.

But rubber boots aren't the only kind. You don't want to go on but you can't stop yourself. Riding boots, you think, with the sinister crop; but that's not too bad, they're foreign and historical. Cowboy boots, two of them, planted apart, stomp, stomp, on main street just before the shot rings out. A spur, in the groin. A man's gotta do, but why this? Jackboots, so highly shined you can see your own face in the right one, as the left one raises itself and the heel comes down on your nose. Now you see rows of them, marching, marching; yours is the street-level view, because you are lying down. Power is the power to smash, two hold your legs, two your arms, the fifth shoves a pointed instrument into you; a bayonet, the neck of a broken bottle, and it's not even wartime, this is a park, with a children's playground, tiny red and yellow horses, it's daytime, men and women stare at you out of their closed car windows. Later the policeman will ask you what you did to provoke this. Boots were not such a bright idea after all.

But just because all rapists are men it doesn't follow that all men are rapists, you tell yourself. You try desperately to retain the image of the man you love and also like, but now it's a sand-coloured plain, no houses left standing anywhere, columns of smoke ascending, trenches filled with no quarter, heads with the faces rotting away, mothers, babies, young boys and girls, men as well, turning to skulls, who did this? Who defines *enemy*? How can you like men?

Still, you continue to believe it can be done. If not all men, at least some, at least two, at least one. It takes an act, of faith. There is his foot, sticking out from under the sheet, asleep, naked as the day he was born. The day he was born. Maybe that's what you have to go back to, in order to trace him here, the journey he took, step by step. In order to begin. Again and again.

Strawberries

The strawberries when I first remember them are not red but blue, that blue flare, before the whitehot part of the wire, sun glancing from the points of waves. It was the heat that made things blue like that, rage, I went into the waste orchard because I did not want to talk to you or even see you, I wanted instead to do something small and useful that I was good at. It was June, there were mosquitoes, I stirred them up as I pushed aside the higher stems, but I didn't care, I was immune, all that adrenalin kept them away, and if not I was in the mood for minor lacerations. I don't get angry like that any more. I almost miss it.

I'd like to say I saw everything through a haze of red; which is not true. Nothing was hazy. Everything was very clear, clearer than usual, my hands with the stained nails, the sunlight falling on the ground through the apple-tree branches, each leaf, each white five petalled yellow centred flower and conical fine-haired dark red multi-seeded dwarf berry rendering itself in dry flat two dimensional detail, like background foliage by one of the crazier Victorian painters, just before the invention of the camera; and at some time during that hour, though not for the whole hour, I forgot what things were called and saw instead what they are.

Him

Every time, when you open the door to him, it's
much the same: as if he's just come from another
planet, he stands there semi-blinded, by the sudden
light, as if you are shedding it, from within, as if he
is his own dark hurtling gravity-free interior and he's
just landed and you are the land. He knows he has to
make his alien greeting and you know it too, it will
be courteous, and awkward because of his difficulties
with the language. *I come in peace*, you want to prompt
him, but don't. He's anxious enough already. It's the
way he inclines his head, looking instead at the floor,
having looked at you first with eyes so unprotected

and candid you couldn't look back. Like many other sad men, he wants only to be allowed. To be taken in.

You're tired of the sadness of men, it's been used on you too often, sadness like a clumsy plumber's wrench, a tool for bludgeoning water. Sadness has been offered as a good reason for you to do all sorts of things. He's not offering it. He's not without sadness but he's no purveyor of his own grief, he's unconscious of it; he's unconscious. He likes watching well-played games.

You want to get fancy, you want to say, he's like a tree or a stone, one of those mute contained objects, but for once you avoid metaphors: there's nothing else you want to change him into. Your years of practice, that skill in metamorphosis, count for nothing here. How many times have you awakened in the moonlight and seen those indigo shadows instead of eyes, hard as if cast by granite, and thought, I'm in bed with a killer? You can crumple all that time up with one hand now and throw it away.

Your worst fear is that you might have missed this. Still, you have to come clean and it angers you; but how can it? Isn't this what you wanted? Isn't this the man through whom all men can be forgiven? Must be forgiven, because now you're beginning to remember the way the others were partly like him.

Hopeless

Today I seem to myself merely sentimental, at the window, looking out at the slush and worrying about the Book of Job. Religion, the burnt heart gripped in its ritual thorns, the chest wall open like a display window. Why are there hookworms? Why are there explosions, on the road, in the wrists, blood hazing the ionosphere?

Forget about tough and competent, I can pour boiling lead from the battlements with one hand, I'm used to it by now, I hardly even look at the scorched faces down there, open mouths with their needle-pointed weasel teeth and all those enraged flags waving around. That's what I do on weekdays, during invasions, but today is Sunday and I'm hopeless, we're hopeless. Hope needs the future tense, which only makes you greedy and a hoarder: the future is what you save up for but like thunder it's only an echo, a reverse dream. Hope is when you expect something more, and what more is there?

Outside, the plague bulges, slops over, flows down the streets and so we stay here, holding on and holding on, to the one small thing which is not yet withering, not yet marked for death, this armful of words, *together, with.* This is as good as it gets, nothing can be better and so there's nothing to hope for, but I do it anyway. In the distance, beyond the war in the midground, there's a river, and some willows, in sunlight, and some hills.

A Parable

I'm in a room with no windows that open and no doors that close, which may sound like an insane asylum but is actually only a room, the room where I'm sitting to write to you once more, one more letter, one more piece of paper, deaf, dumb and blind. When I'm finished I will throw it into the air and as we say it will disappear, but the air will not think so.

I'm listening to your questions. The reason I don't answer them is that they are not questions at all. Is there any answer to a stone or the sun? *What is this for?* you say, to which the only possible reply is that we are not all utilitarians. *Who are you really?* is the question asked by the worm of the apple on the way through. A gnawed core may be the centre but is it the reality?

As for me, I may not be anything at all but the space between your right hand and your left hand when your hands are on my shoulders. I keep your right hand and your left hand apart, through me they also touch. It feels like silence, which is a sound also. I am the time it takes you to think about that. You enter my time, you leave it, I cannot enter or leave, why ask me? You know what it looks like and I don't. Mirrors are no use at all.

Ask me instead who you are: when you walk into this room through the door that isn't there, it's not myself I see but you.

Hand

Your body lies on the floor, with or without you. Your eyes are closed. No good to say you are your body, though this also is true; because at the moment you are not; you are only a fist tightening somewhere at the back of the neck. It's this fist that holds you clenched and pushes you forward with short jabs of pain, it's this fist that drives you through time, along those windowless corridors we know so well, where the yellowish-white light sucks the blood from the surface of your face and your feet in their narrowing shoes hit cement, a thud and then another, clockwork. This fist is what I must open: to let you in.

I begin with the back of the neck, lightly, feeling the involved knot of muscle, in its own grip, a puzzle. A false start, to press too hard here would bruise you. I move to the feet and begin again.

The feet must be taught to see in the dark, because the dark is where they walk. The feet learn quietly; they are wiser than the eyes, they are hard to fool, like stones they are heavy and grave, they desire nothing for themselves, once they have seen they remember. I move my thumbs down between the tendons, push on the deaf white sole, of the imprisoned feet.

This is your body I hold between both of my hands, its eyes closed. Now your body has become a hand that is opening, your body is the hand of a blind man, reaching out into a darkness which may in fact be light; for all you know. Behind your closed eyes the filaments of a tree unwind, take shape, red and purple, blue, a slow glow. This is not a lovers' scenario. This is the journey of the body, its hesitant footsteps as it walks back into its own flesh. I close my own eyes so I can see better where we are going. My hands move forward by knowledge and guess; my hands

106

move you forward. Your eyes are closed but the third eye, the eye of the body, is opening. It floats before you like a ring of blue fire. Now you see into it and through it.

Everlasting

I reach down and what do I come up with? Something early, a small dry white flower. Everlasting, it was called. Picked by the roadside, highway, near a rockface shot through with quartz; on which the sun shone as it rose, lighting up the rock like glass, like an entrance into light. Right then the world was something you could walk through, into.

You could tent then, anywhere, just beside the road, any wide place. The tents were heavy canvas and smelled of tar. The others put the fire out. There were almost no cars; it was because of the war. The war was happening somewhere, and the devil's paintbrushes, red and orange, grew there in clumps, purple vetch, daisies with their heavy smell, tiny black ants on the petals. A stream too, the water brownish and clear.

There was nothing to do, there was all that time, which did not need to be filled. I knelt down, bare skin on the damp ground, and reached into the absence of time and came up with a handful of stems, on their ends the light reflecting from the stream, the dry white flowers, already eternal.

Instructions for the Third Eye

The eye is the organ of vision, and the third eye is no exception to that. Open it and it sees, close it and it doesn't.

Most people have a third eye but they don't trust it. That wasn't really F., standing on the corner, hands in his overcoat pockets, waiting for the light to change: F. died two months ago. It's a trick my eyes played on me, they say. A trick of the light.

I've got nothing against telepathy, said Jane; but the telephone is so much more dependable.

———

What's the difference between vision and a vision? The former relates to something it's assumed you've seen, the latter to something it's assumed you haven't. Language is not always dependable either.

———

If you want to use the third eye you must close the other two. Then breathe evenly; then wait. This sometimes works; on the other hand, sometimes you merely go to sleep. That sometimes works also.

———

When you've had enough practice you don't have to bother with these preliminary steps. You find too that what you see depends partly on what you want to look at and partly on how. As I said, the third eye is only an eye.

———

There are some who resent the third eye. They would have it removed, if they could. They feel it as a parasite, squatting in the centre of the forehead, feeding on the brain.

To them the third eye shows only the worst scenery: the gassed and scorched corpses at the cave-mouth, the gutted babies, the spoor left by generals, and, closer to home, the hearts gone bubonic with jealousy and greed, glinting through the vests and sweaters of anyone at all. Torment, they say and see. The third eye can be merciless, especially when wounded.

———

But someone has to see these things. They exist. Try not to resist the third eye: it knows what it's doing. Leave it alone and it will show you that this truth is not the only truth. One day you will wake up and everything, the stones by the driveway, the brick houses, each brick, each leaf of each tree, your own body, will be glowing from within, lit up, so bright you can hardly look. You will reach out in any direction and you will touch the light itself.

———————

After that there are no more instructions because there is no more choice. You see. You see.

WILDERNESS TIPS

Margaret Atwood

A leathery bog-man transforms an old love affair;
a sweet, gruesome gift is sent to the wife of an ex-lover;
landscape paintings are haunted by the ghost of a young
girl. This dazzling collection of ten short stories takes us
into familiar Atwood territory to reveal the logic of
irrational behaviour and the many textures
lying beneath ordinary life.

'Atwood is a writer of importance, with a deep
understanding of human behaviour, a beautiful understated
style, and rarest of all, a broad scope' Marilyn French

MURDER IN THE DARK

Margaret Atwood

These short fictions and prose poems are beautifully bizarre: bread can no longer be thought of as wholesome comforting loaves; the pretensions of the male chef are subjected to a light roasting; a poisonous brew is concocted by cynical five year olds; and knowing when to stop is of deadly importance in a game of Murder in the Dark.

'Direct, unpretentious, humorous' *Sunday Times*

MORAL DISORDER

Margaret Atwood

EATING FIRE

Margaret Atwood

'Atwood is the quiet Mata Hari, the mysterious,
violent figure . . . who pits herself against the ordered
too-clean world like an arsonist'
Michael Ondaatje

The evolution of Margaret Atwood's poetry illuminates
a major literary talent. Through bus trips and postcards,
wilderness and trivia, she reflects the passion and energy
of a writer intensely engaged with her craft and the world.
In this volume, two previous selections, *Poems 1965–1975*
and *Poems 1976–1986* are presented together with
Morning in the Burned House.

'Detached, ironic, loving by turns . . . poems that
sing off the page and sting'
Michèle Roberts

virago

To buy any of our books and to find out more
about Virago Press and Virago Modern Classics,
our authors and titles, as well as events and
book club forum, visit our websites

www.virago.co.uk
www.littlebrown.co.uk

and follow us on Twitter

@ViragoBooks

To order any Virago titles p & p free in the UK,
please contact our mail order supplier on:

+ 44 (0)1832 737525

Customers not based in the UK should contact
the same number for appropriate postage
and packing costs.